The ABCs of COVID-19

Helping Children Understand the Global Pandemic

Written by Dr. Tasha Thompson-Gray

Illustrated by Stephanie Rogers Carter

Please send requests for bulk orders and special events to
ttkreativeenterprise@gmail.com.

Library of Congress Control Number: 2020917931

Published by P A Reading Press
Calumet City, IL 60409
pareadingpress@gmail.com

Message from the author:

During the global pandemic, I was concerned about my loved ones' safety and survival. Many people were struggling spiritually, mentally, physically, emotionally, and financially. I prayed for people who had the virus, people at risk for contracting the virus, and families who lost loved ones to the virus. I also prayed for the essential workers who put themselves at risk while serving the general public, and I prayed for children. I knew some children did not understand why they could no longer go to school and church. I knew some children did not know why they could not have a traditional birthday celebration, play with their friends, or go to their favorite restaurants. I knew some children did not understand what was going on in the world around them. That is why I wrote this book to help children understand the global pandemic of 2020, known as Covid-19.

This book is dedicated to every child who was impacted by the global pandemic.

Thank you to my children, Tashan and Kristen, for your support and encouragement. A special thank you to my father for teaching me the ABCs when I was a toddler and pushing me to keep learning. In loving memory of my mother and grandparents...

All over the world, people were getting sick from a virus.

Breaking **NEWS**

COVID-19

B

Information about the virus was broadcasted on the news each day.

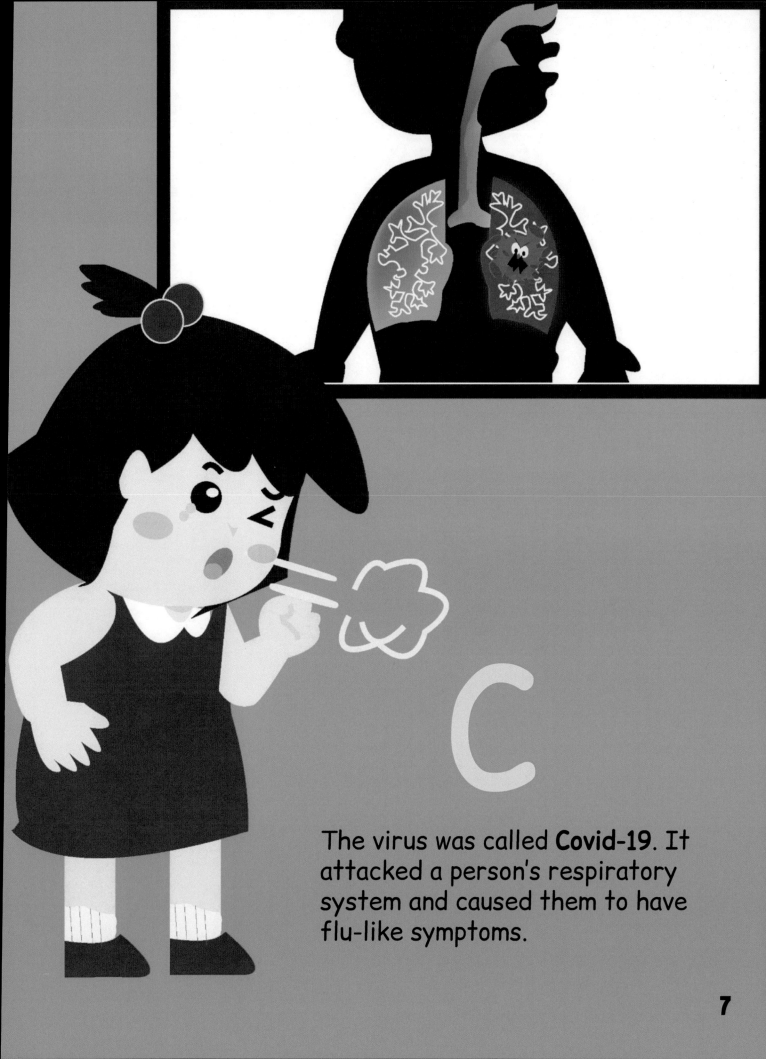

The virus was called **Covid-19**. It attacked a person's respiratory system and caused them to have flu-like symptoms.

D Doctors and nurses treated so many sick
people that the government decided it was
best to close schools and most public places
to help stop the spread of the Covid-19 virus.

Essential businesses like hospitals and grocery stores remained open so people could receive services necessary for survival. Other places like churches, schools, and malls were closed for months.

First responders like doctors, nurses, police officers, and firefighters still had to report to work. Some people worked from home using the Internet.

Schools remained closed, and traditional **graduation** ceremonies were replaced with virtual and drive-by celebrations.

People had to come up with creative ways to celebrate **holidays**, birthdays, and other special occasions. Car parades, virtual parties, and yard decorations were a few of the most popular ways to celebrate.

To avoid getting the virus, some people did things to boost their immune system. A person's **immune system** consists of cells in their body that help keep them from getting sick. Vitamin C, zinc, and turmeric were a few supplements that people took to boost their immune system.

People were not able to go to fun places like beaches, movie theaters, and parks. Almost everyone was concerned about the spread of the Covid-19 virus and **just stayed home.**

Please Stay
6 Feet
Apart

K

The government established restrictions and health precautions to help **keep everyone** safe from the Covid-19 virus. Large gatherings were prohibited. Everyone was encouraged to wash their hands for at least 20 seconds numerous times a day.

Thompson's Groceries

Only a limited number of people could be in the store all at once, so people had to wait in **long lines** outside. Families needed more food than usual, and stores ran out of food and cleaning supplies. Shopping was more like a scavenger hunt.

Face Mask

M

People were required to wear **masks** when they were in public places. The masks covered the person's nose and mouth to prevent the Covid-19 virus from getting inside their body.

N

The Covid-19 virus caused life to be very different. Everyone had to adjust to the "**new normal.**"

Most cities and states had "Stay at Home" orders in place for about 100 days, which meant people did not leave home unless it was necessary. Restaurants were **open for delivery and carryout** only.

Mary's Diner
Open
Delivery and Carryout
ONLY

Breaking **NEWS** Global Pandemic

NOW

All Over the World

COVID-19

P The Covid-19 virus was described as a global **pandemic** because it had spread all over the world. Global pandemics are very rare. The last one happened about 100 years ago.

Doctors asked people to **quarantine** themselves for 14 days if they had symptoms of Covid-19 or had been in contact with someone who had the virus. When a person was under quarantine, they isolated themselves from other people.

Schools were closed for months during the health crisis. Remote learning allowed students to attend school virtually from home. Teachers did their best to remain in contact with their students.

SOCIAL DISTANCING

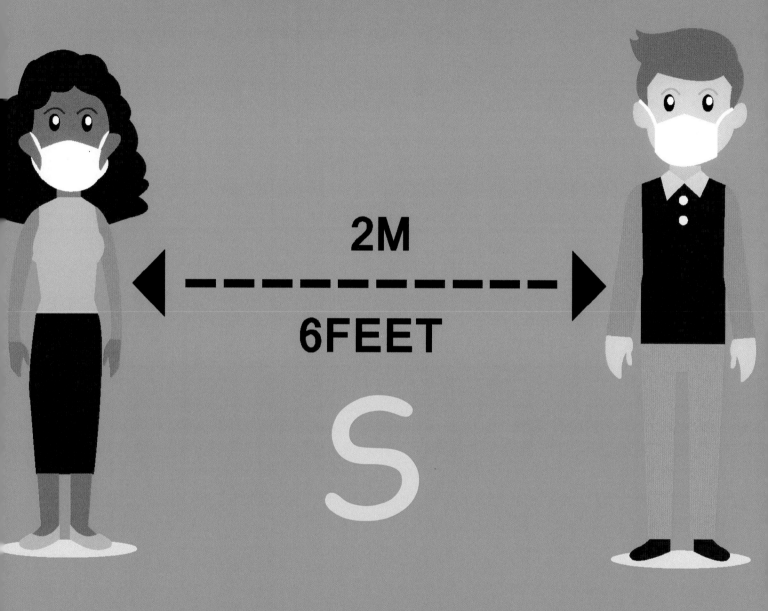

2M

6FEET

S

The government established **social distancing** guidelines to keep everyone safe from Covid-19. Social distancing meant that people limited face-to-face contact with other people and stayed at least six feet apart.

Toilet Paper
SOLD OUT

Toilet paper was out of stock during the global pandemic. No one understood why, so people just made jokes and laughed about it.

U These were **unprecedented times**! No one had ever experienced anything like this before. It was as if the world had come to a halt.

Medical researchers continued to work very hard, trying to create a **vaccine** so people would not continue to get sick from the Covid-19 virus.

Life was **weird** during the global pandemic.
People could not visit their family and friends.
Sporting events and concerts were canceled. It
was bizarre to see so many places closed.

Everyone had to be creative to keep in touch with other people and give a **xenium** to someone. Video calls and conferences were a popular way to interact with other people. Some people started new hobbies, like gardening and painting. Families watched movies, played games, and made funny videos together. There were a lot of challenges and fun events on social media.

The **year 2020** was very different for the entire world. People were not sure if life would ever be the same again.

Thank You
Essential Workers

STAY HOME STAY SAFE

Hair Cuts by
Appointment
Only!!!

Z

However, everyone showed great **zeal**, perseverance, and resilience to stay safe and survive the global pandemic known as Covid-19.

Appendix

The names of the buildings in this book were chosen to pay homage to people and places with significant meaning to the author.

Sims Hospital (page 9): This fictitious hospital was named in honor of the author's great grandfather. He was a licensed pharmacist who owned a pharmacy in Los Angeles, CA.

Sherman Park (page 14): This is a real park located in Chicago, IL, the author's hometown. The author spent a lot of time with friends in this park and participated in sports, dance classes, and day camps hosted by Sherman Park.

Thompson's Groceries (page 16): The author's great, great uncle owned a grocery store in Waterloo, Iowa bearing the same name. Mr. Thompson was half Black and half Irish. He was approved for the loan used to open the store in the 1960s because the banker did not realize that he was Black. The banker even asked Mr. Thompson why he wanted to open a store in the Black neighborhood.

Mary's Diner (page 19): The author's paternal grandmother was an excellent cook who loved to prepare delicious meals and desserts for her family. She also enjoyed serving as a volunteer cook at a local soup kitchen six days a week. The fictitious diner bears her name.

Ivy Rec Center (page 27): The author's father was an athlete during his younger years, and he spent his free time playing basketball and baseball. He had an opportunity to get drafted by the Yankees, but his father urged him to go to college instead.

Thompson Library (page 27): The author's maternal grandparents had shelves of books in their hallway. Her grandfather built the shelves to hold all of the books that her grandmother purchased for the family. The hall of books helped to promote the love of reading in the author.

Made in the USA
Monee, IL
29 December 2020